My Running

Belonging to.

Address _____

_____

_____

_____

Phone _____

Email _____

My Goal:

Run for Fun

Run for Health

Run for Peace

Run for Control

Run for Life

Run for Love

Run for You

Because...

You Can.

About This Log

The Journey Begins:

Using this runners log will help to keep you motivated and accountable for the journey ahead of 100 fantastic runs. Inside, you will find a full page for each run where you can log your stats and write a few words for reflection and motivation.

At the back, there are 4 pages of 'at-a-glace' stats that you can build up over your 100 runs. Also, after completion, there is a little Q and A section for you to fill in on reflection of these 100 runs.

*If you run just once or twice a week, this log will last for a year. If you run every day, it will keep you busy for around 15 weeks.

Log Your:

- Date	- Average Heart Rate
- Run Number	- Average Pace
- Time Started	- Calories Burned
- Time Ended	- Weather Conditions
- Total Time	- Injury Note
- Distance	- Run Summary

Club Membership

If you're a member of a running or athletics club, fill in the contact details below for quick reference.

Club Name: ....
Address: ....
....
Club Contact Details: ....
Membership Number: ....

| Day | | Date | | **Run 1** |

Brief Description of Location & Route

Start Time	End time	Total Time	Distance

Average Heart Rate   Average Pace   Calories Burned

( )   ( )   ( )

Weather Conditions   Any Injuries?

- Mild/Fair   O   Misty   O
- Warm   O   Humid   O
- Hot   O   Sunny   O
- Cold   O   Rain   O
- Icy/Snow   O

How did the run go?

One Word To Summarize This Run   Satisfaction Rating

                                           (1) (2) (3) (4) (5)

| Day | .... | Date | .... |

Run 2

Brief Description of Location & Route

Start Time	End time	Total Time	Distance

Average Heart Rate Average Pace Calories Burned

Weather Conditions

Any Injuries?

Mild/Fair   O   Misty   O
Warm   O   Humid   O
Hot   O   Sunny   O
Cold   O   Rain   O
Icy/Snow   O

How did the run go?

One Word To Summarize This Run   Satisfaction Rating

....   (1) (2) (3) (4) (5)

Day .... Date ....

Run 3

Brief Description of Location & Route

....
....

Start Time	End time	Total Time	Distance

Average Heart Rate   Average Pace   Calories Burned

Weather Conditions   Any Injuries?

Mild/Fair ○   Misty ○   ....
Warm   ○   Humid ○   ....
Hot   ○   Sunny ○   ....
Cold   ○   Rain   ○
Icy/Snow   ○

How did the run go?

....
....
....
....
....

One Word To Summarize This Run   Satisfaction Rating

....   (1) (2) (3) (4) (5)

| Day | .... | Date | .... |

Run 4

Brief Description of Location & Route

Start Time	End time	Total Time	Distance

Average Heart Rate   **Average Pace**   **Calories Burned**

Weather Conditions

- Mild/Fair ○
- Warm ○
- Hot ○
- Cold ○
- Icy/Snow ○

- Misty ○
- Humid ○
- Sunny ○
- Rain ○

Any Injuries?

How did the run go?

One Word To Summarize This Run

....

Satisfaction Rating

(1) (2) (3) (4) (5)

| Day | .... | Date | .... |

Run 5

Brief Description of Location & Route

....
....

Start Time	End time	Total Time	Distance

Average Heart Rate • Average Pace • Calories Burned

Weather Conditions

Mild/Fair ○   Misty ○
Warm   ○   Humid ○
Hot   ○   Sunny ○
Cold   ○   Rain   ○
Icy/Snow   ○

Any Injuries?
....
....
....

How did the run go?

....
....
....
....
....

One Word To Summarize This Run

....

Satisfaction Rating

(1) (2) (3) (4) (5)

| Day | Date |

Brief Description of Location & Route

Run 6

Start Time	End time	Total Time	Distance

Average Heart Rate | Average Pace | Calories Burned

Weather Conditions

Any Injuries?

- Mild/Fair ○
- Warm ○
- Hot ○
- Cold ○
- Icy/Snow ○

- Misty ○
- Humid ○
- Sunny ○
- Rain ○

How did the run go?

One Word To Summarize This Run

Satisfaction Rating

(1) (2) (3) (4) (5)

| Day | Date |

Run 7

Brief Description of Location & Route

Start Time	End time	Total Time	Distance

Average Heart Rate   Average Pace   Calories Burned

Weather Conditions   Any Injuries?

Mild/Fair   O   Misty   O
Warm   O   Humid   O
Hot   O   Sunny   O
Cold   O   Rain   O
Icy/Snow   O

How did the run go?

One Word To Summarize This Run   Satisfaction Rating

                                  (1)   (2)   (3)   (4)   (5)

| Day | | Date | |

Run 8

Brief Description of Location & Route

Start Time	End time	Total Time	Distance

Average Heart Rate | Average Pace | Calories Burned

Weather Conditions

- Mild/Fair ○
- Warm ○
- Hot ○
- Cold ○
- Icy/Snow ○
- Misty ○
- Humid ○
- Sunny ○
- Rain ○

Any Injuries?

How did the run go?

One Word To Summarize This Run

Satisfaction Rating

(1) (2) (3) (4) (5)

Day .... Date ....

Run 9

Brief Description of Location & Route

Start Time	End time	Total Time	Distance

Average Heart Rate   Average Pace   Calories Burned

Weather Conditions

- Mild/Fair   O
- Warm   O
- Hot   O
- Cold   O
- Icy/Snow   O

- Misty   O
- Humid   O
- Sunny   O
- Rain   O

Any Injuries?

How did the run go?

One Word To Summarize This Run

....

Satisfaction Rating

(1)   (2)   (3)   (4)   (5)

Day .... Date ....

Run **10**

Brief Description of Location & Route

Start Time	End time	Total Time	Distance

Average Heart Rate · Average Pace · Calories Burned

Weather Conditions

- Mild/Fair ○
- Warm ○
- Hot ○
- Cold ○
- Icy/Snow ○

- Misty ○
- Humid ○
- Sunny ○
- Rain ○

Any Injuries?

How did the run go?

One Word To Summarize This Run

Satisfaction Rating

(1) (2) (3) (4) (5)

Day .... Date ....

Run 11

Brief Description of Location & Route

....

....

Start Time	End time	Total Time	Distance

Average Heart Rate   Average Pace   Calories Burned

Weather Conditions

Mild/Fair O   Misty   O
Warm   O   Humid   O
Hot   O   Sunny   O
Cold   O   Rain   O
Icy/Snow   O

Any Injuries?

....

....

....

How did the run go?

....
....
....
....
....

One Word To Summarize This Run   Satisfaction Rating

....   (1) (2) (3) (4) (5)

Day	Date

Run 12

Brief Description of Location & Route

Start Time	End time	Total Time	Distance

Average Heart Rate   Average Pace   Calories Burned

Weather Conditions

- Mild/Fair O
- Warm O
- Hot O
- Cold O
- Icy/Snow O

- Misty O
- Humid O
- Sunny O
- Rain O

Any Injuries?

How did the run go?

One Word To Summarize This Run

Satisfaction Rating

(1) (2) (3) (4) (5)

| Day | Date |

Run 13

Brief Description of Location & Route

Start Time	End time	Total Time	Distance

Average Heart Rate   Average Pace   Calories Burned

Weather Conditions

- Mild/Fair ○
- Warm ○
- Hot ○
- Cold ○
- Icy/Snow ○
- Misty ○
- Humid ○
- Sunny ○
- Rain ○

Any Injuries?

How did the run go?

One Word To Summarize This Run

Satisfaction Rating

(1) (2) (3) (4) (5)

| Day | Date |

Run 14

Brief Description of Location & Route

Start Time	End time	Total Time	Distance

Average Heart Rate   Average Pace   Calories Burned

Weather Conditions   Any Injuries?

Mild/Fair   O   Misty   O
Warm   O   Humid   O   ------------------------
Hot   O   Sunny   O   ------------------------
Cold   O   Rain   O   ------------------------
Icy/Snow   O

How did the run go?

One Word To Summarize This Run   Satisfaction Rating

(1) (2) (3) (4) (5)

| Day | .... | Date | .... |

Run 15

Brief Description of Location & Route

Start Time	End time	Total Time	Distance

Average Heart Rate Average Pace Calories Burned

Weather Conditions Any Injuries?

Mild/Fair ○   Misty ○
Warm   ○   Humid ○ --------------------
Hot   ○   Sunny ○ --------------------
Cold   ○   Rain   ○ --------------------
Icy/Snow ○

How did the run go?

One Word To Summarize This Run Satisfaction Rating

-------------- (1) (2) (3) (4) (5)

| Day | Date |

Run 16

Brief Description of Location & Route

Start Time	End time	Total Time	Distance

Average Heart Rate   Average Pace   Calories Burned

Weather Conditions

- Mild/Fair ○
- Warm ○
- Hot ○
- Cold ○
- Icy/Snow ○
- Misty ○
- Humid ○
- Sunny ○
- Rain ○

Any Injuries?

How did the run go?

One Word To Summarize This Run

Satisfaction Rating

(1) (2) (3) (4) (5)

| Day | | Date | |

Run 17

Brief Description of Location & Route

Start Time	End time	Total Time	Distance

Average Heart Rate   Average Pace   Calories Burned

Weather Conditions   **Any Injuries?**

- Mild/Fair ○   Misty ○
- Warm ○   Humid ○
- Hot ○   Sunny ○
- Cold ○   Rain ○
- Icy/Snow ○

How did the run go?

One Word To Summarize This Run   *Satisfaction Rating*

(1) (2) (3) (4) (5)

Day .... Date ....

Run 18

Brief Description of Location & Route

Start Time	End time	Total Time	Distance

Average Heart Rate   Average Pace   Calories Burned

Weather Conditions   *Any Injuries?*

- Mild/Fair ○   Misty ○
- Warm   ○   Humid ○
- Hot   ○   Sunny ○
- Cold   ○   Rain   ○
- Icy/Snow   ○

How did the run go?

One Word To Summarize This Run   *Satisfaction Rating*

....   (1) (2) (3) (4) (5)

| Day | .... | Date | .... |

Run 19

Brief Description of Location & Route

....

....

Start Time	End time	Total Time	Distance

Average Heart Rate   Average Pace   Calories Burned

Weather Conditions   Any Injuries?

- Mild/Fair ○
- Warm ○
- Hot ○
- Cold ○
- Icy/Snow ○
- Misty ○
- Humid ○
- Sunny ○
- Rain ○

....

....

....

How did the run go?

....
....
....
....
....

One Word To Summarize This Run   Satisfaction Rating

(1) (2) (3) (4) (5)

....

Day .... *Date* ....

Run 20

Brief Description of Location & Route

Start Time	End time	Total Time	Distance

Average Heart Rate   *Average Pace*   *Calories Burned*

Weather Conditions   *Any Injuries?*

- Mild/Fair ○   Misty ○
- Warm   ○   Humid ○
- Hot   ○   Sunny ○
- Cold   ○   Rain   ○
- Icy/Snow ○

How did the run go?

One Word To Summarize This Run   *Satisfaction Rating*

....   (1) (2) (3) (4) (5)

Day .... Date ....

Run 21

Brief Description of Location & Route

Start Time	End time	Total Time	Distance

Average Heart Rate Average Pace Calories Burned

Weather Conditions   **Any Injuries?**

- Mild/Fair ○   Misty ○
- Warm ○   Humid ○   ------------------------
- Hot ○   Sunny ○
- Cold ○   Rain ○   ------------------------
- Icy/Snow ○

How did the run go?

One Word To Summarize This Run   **Satisfaction Rating**

....   (1) (2) (3) (4) (5)

| Day | | Date | |

Run 22

Brief Description of Location & Route

Start Time	End time	Total Time	Distance

Average Heart Rate   Average Pace   Calories Burned

Weather Conditions

Mild/Fair   ○   Misty   ○
Warm   ○   Humid   ○
Hot   ○   Sunny   ○
Cold   ○   Rain   ○
Icy/Snow   ○

Any Injuries?

How did the run go?

One Word To Summarize This Run

Satisfaction Rating

(1) (2) (3) (4) (5)

| Day | Date |

Brief Description of Location & Route

Run **23**

Start Time	End time	Total Time	Distance

Average Heart Rate   Average Pace   Calories Burned

Weather Conditions   Any Injuries?

- Mild/Fair ○
- Warm ○
- Hot ○
- Cold ○
- Icy/Snow ○
- Misty ○
- Humid ○
- Sunny ○
- Rain ○

How did the run go?

One Word To Summarize This Run   Satisfaction Rating

(1) (2) (3) (4) (5)

| Day | .... | Date | .... |

Run 24

Brief Description of Location & Route

....

....

Start Time	End time	Total Time	Distance

- Average Heart Rate
- Average Pace
- Calories Burned

Weather Conditions

- Mild/Fair ○
- Warm ○
- Hot ○
- Cold ○
- Icy/Snow ○

- Misty ○
- Humid ○
- Sunny ○
- Rain ○

Any Injuries?

....

....

....

How did the run go?

....
....
....
....
....

One Word To Summarize This Run

....

Satisfaction Rating

(1) (2) (3) (4) (5)

| Day | Date |

Run 25

Brief Description of Location & Route

Start Time	End time	Total Time	Distance

Average Heart Rate Average Pace Calories Burned

Weather Conditions　　　　　　　Any Injuries?

Mild/Fair ○   Misty   ○
Warm   ○   Humid   ○
Hot   ○   Sunny   ○
Cold   ○   Rain   ○
Icy/Snow ○

How did the run go?

One Word To Summarize This Run　　　Satisfaction Rating

　　　　　　　　　　　　　　　　(1) (2) (3) (4) (5)

Day .... Date ....

Run 26

Brief Description of Location & Route

....
....

Start Time	End time	Total Time	Distance

Average Heart Rate · Average Pace · Calories Burned

Weather Conditions

Mild/Fair ○ Misty ○
Warm ○ Humid ○
Hot ○ Sunny ○
Cold ○ Rain ○
Icy/Snow ○

Any Injuries?
....
....
....

How did the run go?

....
....
....
....
....

One Word To Summarize This Run

....

Satisfaction Rating

(1) (2) (3) (4) (5)

| Day | .... | Date | .... |

Run 27

Brief Description of Location & Route

Start Time	End time	Total Time	Distance

Average Heart Rate | Average Pace | Calories Burned

Weather Conditions

Mild/Fair O   Misty   O
Warm   O   Humid   O
Hot   O   Sunny   O
Cold   O   Rain   O
Icy/Snow   O

Any Injuries?

How did the run go?

One Word To Summarize This Run

....

Satisfaction Rating

(1) (2) (3) (4) (5)

| Day | .... | Date | .... |

Run 28

Brief Description of Location & Route

Start Time	End time	Total Time	Distance

Average Heart Rate   Average Pace   Calories Burned

Weather Conditions   *Any Injuries?*

- Mild/Fair O
- Warm O
- Hot O
- Cold O
- Icy/Snow O

- Misty O
- Humid O
- Sunny O
- Rain O

How did the run go?

One Word To Summarize This Run   *Satisfaction Rating*

.... (1) (2) (3) (4) (5)

Day .... Date ....

Run 29

Brief Description of Location & Route

Start Time	End time	Total Time	Distance

Average Heart Rate   Average Pace   Calories Burned

Weather Conditions

- Mild/Fair ○
- Warm ○
- Hot ○
- Cold ○
- Icy/Snow ○

- Misty ○
- Humid ○
- Sunny ○
- Rain ○

Any Injuries?

How did the run go?

One Word To Summarize This Run

Satisfaction Rating

(1) (2) (3) (4) (5)

Day .... Date ....

Run 30

Brief Description of Location & Route

Start Time	End time	Total Time	Distance

Average Heart Rate   Average Pace   Calories Burned

Weather Conditions

Mild/Fair O   Misty   O
Warm   O   Humid   O
Hot   O   Sunny   O
Cold   O   Rain   O
Icy/Snow   O

Any Injuries?

How did the run go?

One Word To Summarize This Run   Satisfaction Rating

....   (1) (2) (3) (4) (5)

Day	Date
....	....

Run 31

Brief Description of Location & Route

Start Time	End time	Total Time	Distance

Average Heart Rate · Average Pace · Calories Burned

( ) ( ) ( )

Weather Conditions   Any Injuries?

- Mild/Fair ○
- Warm   ○
- Hot   ○
- Cold   ○
- Icy/Snow   ○

- Misty   ○
- Humid   ○
- Sunny   ○
- Rain   ○

How did the run go?

One Word To Summarize This Run   Satisfaction Rating

(1) (2) (3) (4) (5)

| Day | | Date | |

Run 32

| Brief Description of Location & Route |

Start Time	End time	Total Time	Distance

Average Heart Rate   Average Pace   Calories Burned

Weather Conditions

- Mild/Fair ○
- Warm ○
- Hot ○
- Cold ○
- Icy/Snow ○

- Misty ○
- Humid ○
- Sunny ○
- Rain ○

Any Injuries?

| How did the run go? |

| One Word To Summarize This Run |

Satisfaction Rating

(1) (2) (3) (4) (5)

| Day | | Date | | Run 33 |

Brief Description of Location & Route

Start Time	End time	Total Time	Distance

Average Heart Rate   **Average Pace**   **Calories Burned**

Weather Conditions

Mild/Fair O   Misty   O
Warm   O   Humid   O
Hot   O   Sunny   O
Cold   O   Rain   O
Icy/Snow   O

Any Injuries?

How did the run go?

One Word To Summarize This Run

Satisfaction Rating

(1) (2) (3) (4) (5)

| Day | .... | Date | .... |

Run 34

Brief Description of Location & Route

Start Time	End time	Total Time	Distance

Average Heart Rate | Average Pace | Calories Burned

Weather Conditions

Mild/Fair ○   Misty   ○
Warm   ○   Humid   ○
Hot   ○   Sunny   ○
Cold   ○   Rain   ○
Icy/Snow   ○

Any Injuries?

How did the run go?

One Word To Summarize This Run

Satisfaction Rating

(1) (2) (3) (4) (5)

| Day | | Date | | Run 35 |

Brief Description of Location & Route

Start Time	End time	Total Time	Distance

Average Heart Rate　　　Average Pace　　　Calories Burned

Weather Conditions　　　　　　　Any Injuries?

Mild/Fair　O　Misty　O
Warm　　　O　Humid　O
Hot　　　　O　Sunny　O
Cold　　　 O　Rain　　O
Icy/Snow　 O

How did the run go?

One Word To Summarize This Run　　Satisfaction Rating

(1)　(2)　(3)　(4)　(5)

| Day | Date |

Run 36

Brief Description of Location & Route

Start Time	End time	Total Time	Distance

Average Heart Rate   Average Pace   Calories Burned

Weather Conditions

- Mild/Fair ○
- Warm ○
- Hot ○
- Cold ○
- Icy/Snow ○

- Misty ○
- Humid ○
- Sunny ○
- Rain ○

Any Injuries?

How did the run go?

One Word To Summarize This Run

Satisfaction Rating

(1) (2) (3) (4) (5)

| Day | Date | | Run 37 |

Brief Description of Location & Route

Start Time	End time	Total Time	Distance

Average Heart Rate	Average Pace	Calories Burned
( )	( )	( )

Weather Conditions

Any Injuries?

- Mild/Fair ○
- Warm ○
- Hot ○
- Cold ○
- Icy/Snow ○
- Misty ○
- Humid ○
- Sunny ○
- Rain ○

How did the run go?

One Word To Summarize This Run

Satisfaction Rating

(1) (2) (3) (4) (5)

| Day | | Date | |

Run 38

Brief Description of Location & Route

Start Time	End time	Total Time	Distance

Average Heart Rate Average Pace Calories Burned

Weather Conditions

- Mild/Fair ○
- Warm ○
- Hot ○
- Cold ○
- Icy/Snow ○

- Misty ○
- Humid ○
- Sunny ○
- Rain ○

Any Injuries?

How did the run go?

One Word To Summarize This Run

Satisfaction Rating

(1) (2) (3) (4) (5)

| Day | .... | Date | .... |

Run 39

Brief Description of Location & Route

....
....

Start Time	End time	Total Time	Distance

Average Heart Rate   Average Pace   Calories Burned

Weather Conditions

Mild/Fair   O   Misty   O
Warm   O   Humid   O
Hot   O   Sunny   O
Cold   O   Rain   O
Icy/Snow   O

Any Injuries?

....
....
....

How did the run go?

....
....
....
....
....

One Word To Summarize This Run

....

Satisfaction Rating

(1) (2) (3) (4) (5)

| Day | | Date | | Run 40 |

Brief Description of Location & Route

Start Time	End time	Total Time	Distance

Average Heart Rate Average Pace Calories Burned

Weather Conditions Any Injuries?

- Mild/Fair ○   Misty ○
- Warm ○   Humid ○
- Hot ○   Sunny ○
- Cold ○   Rain ○
- Icy/Snow ○

How did the run go?

One Word To Summarize This Run   Satisfaction Rating

(1) (2) (3) (4) (5)

| Day | | Date | |

Run 41

Brief Description of Location & Route

Start Time	End time	Total Time	Distance

Average Heart Rate   Average Pace   Calories Burned

Weather Conditions   Any Injuries?

Mild/Fair ○   Misty   ○
Warm   ○   Humid   ○   ------------------
Hot   ○   Sunny   ○
Cold   ○   Rain   ○   ------------------
Icy/Snow   ○

How did the run go?

One Word To Summarize This Run   Satisfaction Rating

(1) (2) (3) (4) (5)

Day .... Date ....

Run 42

Brief Description of Location & Route

Start Time	End time	Total Time	Distance

Average Heart Rate   Average Pace   Calories Burned

Weather Conditions   Any Injuries?

Mild/Fair   ○   Misty   ○
Warm   ○   Humid   ○   ------------------------
Hot   ○   Sunny   ○
Cold   ○   Rain   ○   ------------------------
Icy/Snow   ○

How did the run go?

One Word To Summarize This Run   Satisfaction Rating

                                    (1) (2) (3) (4) (5)
....

Day .... Date ....

Run 43

Brief Description of Location & Route

Start Time	End time	Total Time	Distance

Average Heart Rate Average Pace Calories Burned

Weather Conditions

Mild/Fair ○ Misty ○
Warm ○ Humid ○
Hot ○ Sunny ○
Cold ○ Rain ○
Icy/Snow ○

Any Injuries?

How did the run go?

One Word To Summarize This Run

Satisfaction Rating

(1) (2) (3) (4) (5)

| Day | | Date | |

Run 44

Brief Description of Location & Route

Start Time	End time	Total Time	Distance

Average Heart Rate   Average Pace   Calories Burned

Weather Conditions

Mild/Fair   O   Misty   O
Warm   O   Humid   O
Hot   O   Sunny   O
Cold   O   Rain   O
Icy/Snow   O

Any Injuries?

How did the run go?

One Word To Summarize This Run

Satisfaction Rating

(1)   (2)   (3)   (4)   (5)

Day	Date		Run
			45

Brief Description of Location & Route

Start Time	End time	Total Time	Distance

Average Heart Rate · Average Pace · Calories Burned

Weather Conditions   *Any Injuries?*

- Mild/Fair ○   Misty   ○
- Warm   ○   Humid   ○
- Hot   ○   Sunny   ○
- Cold   ○   Rain   ○
- Icy/Snow   ○

How did the run go?

One Word To Summarize This Run   *Satisfaction Rating*

----------------------   (1) (2) (3) (4) (5)

Day	Date

Run 46

Brief Description of Location & Route

Start Time	End time	Total Time	Distance

Average Heart Rate   Average Pace   Calories Burned

Weather Conditions

- Mild/Fair ○
- Warm ○
- Hot ○
- Cold ○
- Icy/Snow ○

- Misty ○
- Humid ○
- Sunny ○
- Rain ○

Any Injuries?

How did the run go?

One Word To Summarize This Run

Satisfaction Rating

(1) (2) (3) (4) (5)

| Day | | Date | |

Run 47

| Brief Description of Location & Route |

Start Time	End time	Total Time	Distance

Average Heart Rate   Average Pace   Calories Burned

( )   ( )   ( )

| Weather Conditions | Any Injuries?

Mild/Fair   O   Misty   O   ----------------------------
Warm   O   Humid   O
Hot   O   Sunny   O   ----------------------------
Cold   O   Rain   O
Icy/Snow   O   ----------------------------

| How did the run go? |

| One Word To Summarize This Run | Satisfaction Rating

                                            (1) (2) (3) (4) (5)

| Day | | Date | |

Run 48

Brief Description of Location & Route

Start Time	End time	Total Time	Distance

Average Heart Rate   Average Pace   Calories Burned

Weather Conditions

- Mild/Fair ○
- Warm   ○
- Hot   ○
- Cold   ○
- Icy/Snow   ○

- Misty   ○
- Humid   ○
- Sunny   ○
- Rain   ○

Any Injuries?

How did the run go?

One Word To Summarize This Run

Satisfaction Rating

(1) (2) (3) (4) (5)

| Day | Date | Run 49 |

Brief Description of Location & Route

Start Time	End time	Total Time	Distance

Average Heart Rate   Average Pace   Calories Burned

Weather Conditions   Any Injuries?

- Mild/Fair ○
- Warm ○
- Hot ○
- Cold ○
- Icy/Snow ○

- Misty ○
- Humid ○
- Sunny ○
- Rain ○

How did the run go?

One Word To Summarize This Run   Satisfaction Rating

(1)   (2)   (3)   (4)   (5)

| Day | Date |

Brief Description of Location & Route

Run 50

| Start Time | End time | Total Time | Distance |

Average Heart Rate   Average Pace   Calories Burned

Weather Conditions   Any Injuries?

- Mild/Fair   ○   Misty   ○
- Warm   ○   Humid   ○
- Hot   ○   Sunny   ○
- Cold   ○   Rain   ○
- Icy/Snow   ○

How did the run go?

One Word To Summarize This Run   Satisfaction Rating

(1) (2) (3) (4) (5)

| Day | .... | Date | .... |

Run 51

Brief Description of Location & Route

....

....

Start Time	End time	Total Time	Distance

Average Heart Rate   Average Pace   Calories Burned

Weather Conditions   Any Injuries?

- Mild/Fair   O   Misty   O
- Warm   O   Humid   O
- Hot   O   Sunny   O
- Cold   O   Rain   O
- Icy/Snow   O

....

....

....

How did the run go?

....
....
....
....
....

One Word To Summarize This Run   Satisfaction Rating

....   (1)   (2)   (3)   (4)   (5)

| Day | Date |

Run 52

Brief Description of Location & Route

Start Time	End time	Total Time	Distance

Average Heart Rate   Average Pace   Calories Burned

Weather Conditions   Any Injuries?

Mild/Fair   ○   Misty   ○
Warm   ○   Humid   ○   ------------------------
Hot   ○   Sunny   ○   ------------------------
Cold   ○   Rain   ○   ------------------------
Icy/Snow   ○

How did the run go?

One Word To Summarize This Run   Satisfaction Rating

                                        (1) (2) (3) (4) (5)

Day .... Date ....

Brief Description of Location & Route

Run
53

Start Time	End time	Total Time	Distance

Average Heart Rate   Average Pace   Calories Burned

Weather Conditions

Mild/Fair O   Misty   O
Warm   O   Humid   O
Hot   O   Sunny   O
Cold   O   Rain   O
Icy/Snow   O

Any Injuries?

How did the run go?

One Word To Summarize This Run   Satisfaction Rating

(1) (2) (3) (4) (5)

| Day | .... | Date | .... |

Run 54

Brief Description of Location & Route

Start Time	End time	Total Time	Distance

Average Heart Rate   Average Pace   Calories Burned

Weather Conditions   *Any Injuries?*

- Mild/Fair ○   Misty   ○
- Warm   ○   Humid   ○
- Hot   ○   Sunny   ○
- Cold   ○   Rain   ○
- Icy/Snow   ○

How did the run go?

One Word To Summarize This Run   *Satisfaction Rating*

....   (1) (2) (3) (4) (5)

| Day | | Date | |

Run 55

Brief Description of Location & Route

Start Time	End time	Total Time	Distance

Average Heart Rate   Average Pace   Calories Burned

Weather Conditions   Any Injuries?

- Mild/Fair ○   Misty ○
- Warm ○   Humid ○
- Hot ○   Sunny ○
- Cold ○   Rain ○
- Icy/Snow ○

How did the run go?

One Word To Summarize This Run   *Satisfaction Rating*

(1) (2) (3) (4) (5)

| Day | | Date | |

Run 56

| Brief Description of Location & Route |

| Start Time | End time | Total Time | Distance |

Average Heart Rate   Average Pace   Calories Burned

| Weather Conditions | Any Injuries?

Mild/Fair   ○   Misty   ○
Warm   ○   Humid   ○   ----
Hot   ○   Sunny   ○   ----
Cold   ○   Rain   ○   ----
Icy/Snow   ○

| How did the run go? |

| One Word To Summarize This Run | Satisfaction Rating

(1) (2) (3) (4) (5)

| Day | Date | Run 57 |

Brief Description of Location & Route

Start Time	End time	Total Time	Distance

Average Heart Rate   Average Pace   Calories Burned

Weather Conditions   Any Injuries?

Mild/Fair   ○   Misty   ○
Warm   ○   Humid   ○   ----------------------
Hot   ○   Sunny   ○
Cold   ○   Rain   ○   ----------------------
Icy/Snow   ○

How did the run go?

One Word To Summarize This Run   Satisfaction Rating

                                          (1) (2) (3) (4) (5)

Day .... Date ....

Brief Description of Location & Route

Run 58

Start Time	End time	Total Time	Distance

Average Heart Rate   Average Pace   Calories Burned

Weather Conditions   Any Injuries?

Mild/Fair   O   Misty   O
Warm   O   Humid   O   ------------------------------
Hot   O   Sunny   O
Cold   O   Rain   O   ------------------------------
Icy/Snow   O

How did the run go?

One Word To Summarize This Run   Satisfaction Rating

....   (1) (2) (3) (4) (5)

Day .... Date ....

Brief Description of Location & Route

Run **59**

Start Time	End time	Total Time	Distance

Average Heart Rate　　　Average Pace　　　Calories Burned

Weather Conditions　　　　　Any Injuries?

Mild/Fair　O　Misty　O
Warm　　　O　Humid　O
Hot　　　　O　Sunny　O
Cold　　　 O　Rain　 O
Icy/Snow　 O

How did the run go?

One Word To Summarize This Run　　Satisfaction Rating

　　　　　　　　　　　　　　　　(1) (2) (3) (4) (5)

....

| Day | Date |

Run 60

Brief Description of Location & Route

Start Time	End time	Total Time	Distance

Average Heart Rate | Average Pace | Calories Burned

Weather Conditions

- Mild/Fair ○
- Warm ○
- Hot ○
- Cold ○
- Icy/Snow ○

- Misty ○
- Humid ○
- Sunny ○
- Rain ○

Any Injuries?

How did the run go?

One Word To Summarize This Run

Satisfaction Rating

(1) (2) (3) (4) (5)

Day .... Date ....

Brief Description of Location & Route

Run **61**

Start Time	End time	Total Time	Distance

Average Heart Rate   Average Pace   Calories Burned

Weather Conditions   Any Injuries?

- Mild/Fair ○   Misty ○
- Warm ○   Humid ○
- Hot ○   Sunny ○
- Cold ○   Rain ○
- Icy/Snow ○

How did the run go?

One Word To Summarize This Run   Satisfaction Rating

(1) (2) (3) (4) (5)

....

| Day | | Date | |

Run 62

| Brief Description of Location & Route |

Start Time	End time	Total Time	Distance

Average Heart Rate   Average Pace   Calories Burned

Weather Conditions

- Mild/Fair O
- Warm O
- Hot O
- Cold O
- Icy/Snow O
- Misty O
- Humid O
- Sunny O
- Rain O

Any Injuries?

| How did the run go? |

| One Word To Summarize This Run |

Satisfaction Rating

(1) (2) (3) (4) (5)

| Day | .... | Date | .... |

Run 63

Brief Description of Location & Route

Start Time	End time	Total Time	Distance

Average Heart Rate	Average Pace	Calories Burned
○	○	○

Weather Conditions **Any Injuries?**

- Mild/Fair ○   Misty ○
- Warm ○   Humid ○
- Hot ○   Sunny ○
- Cold ○   Rain ○
- Icy/Snow ○

How did the run go?

One Word To Summarize This Run   **Satisfaction Rating**

....   (1) (2) (3) (4) (5)

| Day | | Date | |

Run 64

Brief Description of Location & Route

Start Time	End time	Total Time	Distance

Average Heart Rate | Average Pace | Calories Burned

Weather Conditions

- Mild/Fair ○
- Warm ○
- Hot ○
- Cold ○
- Icy/Snow ○
- Misty ○
- Humid ○
- Sunny ○
- Rain ○

Any Injuries?

How did the run go?

One Word To Summarize This Run

Satisfaction Rating

(1) (2) (3) (4) (5)

| Day | | Date | |

Run 65

Brief Description of Location & Route

Start Time	End time	Total Time	Distance

Average Heart Rate — Average Pace — Calories Burned

Weather Conditions

- Mild/Fair ○
- Warm ○
- Hot ○
- Cold ○
- Icy/Snow ○

- Misty ○
- Humid ○
- Sunny ○
- Rain ○

Any Injuries?

How did the run go?

One Word To Summarize This Run

Satisfaction Rating

(1) (2) (3) (4) (5)

| Day | Date | **Run 66** |

Brief Description of Location & Route

Start Time	End time	Total Time	Distance

Average Heart Rate · Average Pace · Calories Burned

Weather Conditions

- Mild/Fair ○
- Warm ○
- Hot ○
- Cold ○
- Icy/Snow ○

- Misty ○
- Humid ○
- Sunny ○
- Rain ○

Any Injuries?

How did the run go?

One Word To Summarize This Run

Satisfaction Rating

(1) (2) (3) (4) (5)

| Day | Date |

Brief Description of Location & Route

Run 67

Start Time	End time	Total Time	Distance

Average Heart Rate | Average Pace | Calories Burned

Weather Conditions

Any Injuries?

- Mild/Fair ○
- Warm ○
- Hot ○
- Cold ○
- Icy/Snow ○

- Misty ○
- Humid ○
- Sunny ○
- Rain ○

How did the run go?

One Word To Summarize This Run

Satisfaction Rating

(1) (2) (3) (4) (5)

Day .... Date ....

Run 68

Brief Description of Location & Route

Start Time	End time	Total Time	Distance

Average Heart Rate   Average Pace   Calories Burned

Weather Conditions

Mild/Fair   O   Misty   O
Warm   O   Humid   O
Hot   O   Sunny   O
Cold   O   Rain   O
Icy/Snow   O

Any Injuries?

How did the run go?

One Word To Summarize This Run   **Satisfaction Rating**

....   (1) (2) (3) (4) (5)

Day .... Date ....

Run 69

Brief Description of Location & Route

Start Time	End time	Total Time	Distance

Average Heart Rate   Average Pace   Calories Burned

Weather Conditions   Any Injuries?

- Mild/Fair ○
- Warm ○
- Hot ○
- Cold ○
- Icy/Snow ○

- Misty ○
- Humid ○
- Sunny ○
- Rain ○

How did the run go?

One Word To Summarize This Run   Satisfaction Rating

(1)   (2)   (3)   (4)   (5)

....

Day .... Date ....

Brief Description of Location & Route

Run **70**

Start Time	End time	Total Time	Distance

Average Heart Rate   Average Pace   Calories Burned

Weather Conditions   *Any Injuries?*

Mild/Fair ○   Misty   ○
Warm   ○   Humid   ○   ------------------------
Hot   ○   Sunny   ○
Cold   ○   Rain   ○   ------------------------
Icy/Snow   ○

How did the run go?

One Word To Summarize This Run   *Satisfaction Rating*

....   (1) (2) (3) (4) (5)

| Day | | Date | |

Run 71

Brief Description of Location & Route

Start Time	End time	Total Time	Distance

Average Heart Rate — Average Pace — Calories Burned

Weather Conditions

- Mild/Fair   ○
- Warm   ○
- Hot   ○
- Cold   ○
- Icy/Snow   ○

- Misty   ○
- Humid   ○
- Sunny   ○
- Rain   ○

Any Injuries?

How did the run go?

One Word To Summarize This Run

Satisfaction Rating

(1) (2) (3) (4) (5)

| Day | Date |

Brief Description of Location & Route

Run 72

| Start Time | End time | Total Time | Distance |

Average Heart Rate Average Pace Calories Burned

Weather Conditions   Any Injuries?

- Mild/Fair ○   Misty ○
- Warm ○   Humid ○
- Hot ○   Sunny ○
- Cold ○   Rain ○
- Icy/Snow ○

How did the run go?

One Word To Summarize This Run   Satisfaction Rating

(1) (2) (3) (4) (5)

| Day | Date |

Run 73

Brief Description of Location & Route

Start Time	End time	Total Time	Distance

Average Heart Rate | Average Pace | Calories Burned

Weather Conditions

- ○ Mild/Fair
- ○ Warm
- ○ Hot
- ○ Cold
- ○ Icy/Snow
- ○ Misty
- ○ Humid
- ○ Sunny
- ○ Rain

Any Injuries?

How did the run go?

One Word To Summarize This Run

Satisfaction Rating

(1) (2) (3) (4) (5)

| Day | Date |

Brief Description of Location & Route

Run
74

Start Time	End time	Total Time	Distance

Average Heart Rate   Average Pace   Calories Burned

Weather Conditions   *Any Injuries?*

- Mild/Fair   ○   Misty   ○
- Warm   ○   Humid   ○
- Hot   ○   Sunny   ○
- Cold   ○   Rain   ○
- Icy/Snow   ○

How did the run go?

One Word To Summarize This Run   *Satisfaction Rating*

(1) (2) (3) (4) (5)

Day	Date

Run 75

Brief Description of Location & Route

Start Time	End time	Total Time	Distance

- Average Heart Rate
- Average Pace
- Calories Burned

Weather Conditions

- Mild/Fair ○
- Warm ○
- Hot ○
- Cold ○
- Icy/Snow ○

- Misty ○
- Humid ○
- Sunny ○
- Rain ○

Any Injuries?

How did the run go?

One Word To Summarize This Run

Satisfaction Rating

(1) (2) (3) (4) (5)

Day .... Date ....

Brief Description of Location & Route

Run **76**

Start Time	End time	Total Time	Distance

Average Heart Rate   Average Pace   Calories Burned

Weather Conditions

Mild/Fair ○   Misty   ○
Warm   ○   Humid   ○
Hot   ○   Sunny   ○
Cold   ○   Rain   ○
Icy/Snow   ○

Any Injuries?

How did the run go?

One Word To Summarize This Run   **Satisfaction Rating**

....   (1) (2) (3) (4) (5)

| Day | .... | Date | .... |

Run 77

Brief Description of Location & Route

Start Time	End time	Total Time	Distance

Average Heart Rate   Average Pace   Calories Burned

Weather Conditions   **Any Injuries?**

Mild/Fair   O   Misty   O
Warm   O   Humid   O
Hot   O   Sunny   O
Cold   O   Rain   O
Icy/Snow   O

How did the run go?

One Word To Summarize This Run   **Satisfaction Rating**

....

(1)   (2)   (3)   (4)   (5)

| Day | Date | Run 78 |

Brief Description of Location & Route

Start Time	End time	Total Time	Distance

Average Heart Rate   Average Pace   Calories Burned

Weather Conditions

- Mild/Fair ○
- Warm ○
- Hot ○
- Cold ○
- Icy/Snow ○

- Misty ○
- Humid ○
- Sunny ○
- Rain ○

Any Injuries?

How did the run go?

One Word To Summarize This Run

Satisfaction Rating

(1) (2) (3) (4) (5)

Day .... Date ....

Run 79

Brief Description of Location & Route

Start Time	End time	Total Time	Distance

Average Heart Rate   Average Pace   Calories Burned

Weather Conditions   Any Injuries?

Mild/Fair   ○   Misty   ○
Warm   ○   Humid   ○   --------------------
Hot   ○   Sunny   ○
Cold   ○   Rain   ○   --------------------
Icy/Snow   ○

How did the run go?

One Word To Summarize This Run   Satisfaction Rating

                                      (1) (2) (3) (4) (5)

....

| Day | | Date | | Run 80 |

Brief Description of Location & Route

Start Time	End time	Total Time	Distance

Average Heart Rate Average Pace Calories Burned

Weather Conditions Any Injuries?

Mild/Fair ○ Misty ○
Warm ○ Humid ○
Hot ○ Sunny ○
Cold ○ Rain ○
Icy/Snow ○

How did the run go?

One Word To Summarize This Run Satisfaction Rating

 (1) (2) (3) (4) (5)

| Day | .... | Date | .... |

Run 81

Brief Description of Location & Route

Start Time	End time	Total Time	Distance

Average Heart Rate   Average Pace   Calories Burned

Weather Conditions   **Any Injuries?**

- Mild/Fair ○   Misty ○
- Warm   ○   Humid ○
- Hot   ○   Sunny ○
- Cold   ○   Rain   ○
- Icy/Snow ○

How did the run go?

One Word To Summarize This Run   **Satisfaction Rating**

(1) (2) (3) (4) (5)

....

| Day | | Date | | Run 82 |

Brief Description of Location & Route

Start Time	End time	Total Time	Distance

Average Heart Rate Average Pace Calories Burned

Weather Conditions

- Mild/Fair ○
- Warm ○
- Hot ○
- Cold ○
- Icy/Snow ○

- Misty ○
- Humid ○
- Sunny ○
- Rain ○

Any Injuries?

How did the run go?

One Word To Summarize This Run

Satisfaction Rating

(1) (2) (3) (4) (5)

| Day | | Date | |

Run 83

Brief Description of Location & Route

Start Time	End time	Total Time	Distance

Average Heart Rate Average Pace Calories Burned

Weather Conditions

- Mild/Fair ○
- Warm ○
- Hot ○
- Cold ○
- Icy/Snow ○

- Misty ○
- Humid ○
- Sunny ○
- Rain ○

Any Injuries?

How did the run go?

One Word To Summarize This Run

Satisfaction Rating

(1) (2) (3) (4) (5)

Day	Date

Brief Description of Location & Route

Run 84

Start Time	End time	Total Time	Distance

Average Heart Rate Average Pace Calories Burned

Weather Conditions

- Mild/Fair ○
- Warm ○
- Hot ○
- Cold ○
- Icy/Snow ○
- Misty ○
- Humid ○
- Sunny ○
- Rain ○

Any Injuries?

How did the run go?

One Word To Summarize This Run

Satisfaction Rating

1   2   3   4   5

Day .... Date ....

Run 85

Brief Description of Location & Route

Start Time	End time	Total Time	Distance

Average Heart Rate   Average Pace   Calories Burned

Weather Conditions   Any Injuries?

- Mild/Fair O
- Warm O
- Hot O
- Cold O
- Icy/Snow O

- Misty O
- Humid O
- Sunny O
- Rain O

How did the run go?

One Word To Summarize This Run   Satisfaction Rating

(1)   (2)   (3)   (4)   (5)

....

| Day | .... | Date | .... |

Run 86

Brief Description of Location & Route

Start Time	End time	Total Time	Distance

Average Heart Rate   Average Pace   Calories Burned

○   ○   ○

Weather Conditions   *Any Injuries?*

Mild/Fair ○   Misty   ○
Warm   ○   Humid   ○   ------------------------
Hot   ○   Sunny   ○
Cold   ○   Rain   ○   ------------------------
Icy/Snow   ○

How did the run go?

One Word To Summarize This Run   *Satisfaction Rating*

....   (1) (2) (3) (4) (5)

Day	Date		Run
			87

Brief Description of Location & Route

Start Time	End time	Total Time	Distance

Average Heart Rate   Average Pace   Calories Burned

( )   ( )   ( )

Weather Conditions   **Any Injuries?**

Mild/Fair   O   Misty   O   _____
Warm   O   Humid   O
Hot   O   Sunny   O   _____
Cold   O   Rain   O
Icy/Snow   O   _____

How did the run go?

One Word To Summarize This Run   Satisfaction Rating

_____   (1) (2) (3) (4) (5)

Day .... Date ....

Brief Description of Location & Route

Run **88**

Start Time	End time	Total Time	Distance

Average Heart Rate Average Pace Calories Burned

Weather Conditions Any Injuries?

Mild/Fair O   Misty   O
Warm   O   Humid   O   ----------------------
Hot   O   Sunny   O
Cold   O   Rain   O   ----------------------
Icy/Snow O

How did the run go?

One Word To Summarize This Run   Satisfaction Rating

....   (1) (2) (3) (4) (5)

| Day | .... | Date | .... |

Run 89

Brief Description of Location & Route

Start Time	End time	Total Time	Distance

Average Heart Rate   Average Pace   Calories Burned

Weather Conditions

- ○ Mild/Fair
- ○ Warm
- ○ Hot
- ○ Cold
- ○ Icy/Snow

- ○ Misty
- ○ Humid
- ○ Sunny
- ○ Rain

Any Injuries?

How did the run go?

One Word To Summarize This Run

....

Satisfaction Rating

(1) (2) (3) (4) (5)

Day .... Date ....

Run 90

Brief Description of Location & Route

Start Time	End time	Total Time	Distance

Average Heart Rate   Average Pace   Calories Burned

Weather Conditions   Any Injuries?

Mild/Fair O   Misty   O
Warm   O   Humid   O   ------------------
Hot   O   Sunny   O   ------------------
Cold   O   Rain   O   ------------------
Icy/Snow   O

How did the run go?

One Word To Summarize This Run   Satisfaction Rating

....   (1) (2) (3) (4) (5)

Day .... Date ....

Brief Description of Location & Route

Run
91

Start Time	End time	Total Time	Distance

Average Heart Rate   Average Pace   Calories Burned

Weather Conditions   Any Injuries?

Mild/Fair   O   Misty   O
Warm   O   Humid   O
Hot   O   Sunny   O
Cold   O   Rain   O
Icy/Snow   O

How did the run go?

One Word To Summarize This Run   Satisfaction Rating

(1)   (2)   (3)   (4)   (5)

| Day | | Date | |

Run 92

Brief Description of Location & Route

Start Time	End time	Total Time	Distance

Average Heart Rate   Average Pace   Calories Burned

Weather Conditions

- Mild/Fair ○
- Warm ○
- Hot ○
- Cold ○
- Icy/Snow ○

- Misty ○
- Humid ○
- Sunny ○
- Rain ○

Any Injuries?

How did the run go?

One Word To Summarize This Run

Satisfaction Rating

(1) (2) (3) (4) (5)

| Day | | Date | |

Run 93

Brief Description of Location & Route

Start Time	End time	Total Time	Distance

Average Heart Rate   Average Pace   Calories Burned

Weather Conditions

Mild/Fair   O   Misty   O
Warm   O   Humid   O
Hot   O   Sunny   O
Cold   O   Rain   O
Icy/Snow   O

Any Injuries?

How did the run go?

One Word To Summarize This Run

Satisfaction Rating

(1)   (2)   (3)   (4)   (5)

| Day | .... | Date | .... |

Run 94

Brief Description of Location & Route

Start Time	End time	Total Time	Distance

Average Heart Rate   Average Pace   Calories Burned

Weather Conditions   *Any Injuries?*

Mild/Fair   O   Misty   O
Warm   O   Humid   O
Hot   O   Sunny   O
Cold   O   Rain   O
Icy/Snow   O

How did the run go?

One Word To Summarize This Run   *Satisfaction Rating*

(1) (2) (3) (4) (5)

....

| Day | Date |

Run 95

Brief Description of Location & Route

Start Time	End time	Total Time	Distance

| Average Heart Rate | Average Pace | Calories Burned |

Weather Conditions

- Mild/Fair ○
- Warm ○
- Hot ○
- Cold ○
- Icy/Snow ○

- Misty ○
- Humid ○
- Sunny ○
- Rain ○

Any Injuries?

How did the run go?

One Word To Summarize This Run

Satisfaction Rating

(1) (2) (3) (4) (5)

| Day | | Date | |

Run 96

Brief Description of Location & Route

Start Time	End time	Total Time	Distance

Average Heart Rate   Average Pace   Calories Burned

Weather Conditions   *Any Injuries?*

- Mild/Fair O
- Warm O
- Hot O
- Cold O
- Icy/Snow O
- Misty O
- Humid O
- Sunny O
- Rain O

How did the run go?

One Word To Summarize This Run   *Satisfaction Rating*

(1) (2) (3) (4) (5)

| Day | | Date | |

Run 97

Brief Description of Location & Route

Start Time	End time	Total Time	Distance

Average Heart Rate　　　Average Pace　　　Calories Burned

Weather Conditions　　　　　**Any Injuries?**

- Mild/Fair ○
- Warm ○
- Hot ○
- Cold ○
- Icy/Snow ○
- Misty ○
- Humid ○
- Sunny ○
- Rain ○

How did the run go?

One Word To Summarize This Run　　　**Satisfaction Rating**

(1)　(2)　(3)　(4)　(5)

| Day | Date |

Run 98

Brief Description of Location & Route

Start Time	End time	Total Time	Distance

Average Heart Rate   Average Pace   Calories Burned

( )   ( )   ( )

Weather Conditions   **Any Injuries?**

Mild/Fair   O   Misty   O   ------------------------------
Warm   O   Humid   O   ------------------------------
Hot   O   Sunny   O   ------------------------------
Cold   O   Rain   O
Icy/Snow   O

How did the run go?

One Word To Summarize This Run   **Satisfaction Rating**

------------------   (1) (2) (3) (4) (5)

Day	Date

Run 99

Brief Description of Location & Route

Start Time	End time	Total Time	Distance

Average Heart Rate   Average Pace   Calories Burned

Weather Conditions

- Mild/Fair ○
- Warm ○
- Hot ○
- Cold ○
- Icy/Snow ○

- Misty ○
- Humid ○
- Sunny ○
- Rain ○

Any Injuries?

How did the run go?

One Word To Summarize This Run

Satisfaction Rating

(1) (2) (3) (4) (5)

| Day | .... | Date | .... |

Run 100

Brief Description of Location & Route

Start Time	End time	Total Time	Distance

Average Heart Rate | Average Pace | Calories Burned

Weather Conditions

Mild/Fair   ○   Misty   ○
Warm   ○   Humid   ○
Hot   ○   Sunny   ○
Cold   ○   Rain   ○
Icy/Snow   ○

Any Injuries?

How did the run go?

One Word To Summarize This Run

Satisfaction Rating

(1)   (2)   (3)   (4)   (5)

At-A-Glance Records

Run	Date	Distance	Time	Pace	Av. HR	Kcal	Satisfaction
1							☆☆☆☆☆
2							☆☆☆☆☆
3							☆☆☆☆☆
4							☆☆☆☆☆
5							☆☆☆☆☆
6							☆☆☆☆☆
7							☆☆☆☆☆
8							☆☆☆☆☆
9							☆☆☆☆☆
10							☆☆☆☆☆
11							☆☆☆☆☆
12							☆☆☆☆☆
13							☆☆☆☆☆
14							☆☆☆☆☆
15							☆☆☆☆☆
16							☆☆☆☆☆
17							☆☆☆☆☆
18							☆☆☆☆☆
19							☆☆☆☆☆
20							☆☆☆☆☆
21							☆☆☆☆☆
22							☆☆☆☆☆
23							☆☆☆☆☆
24							☆☆☆☆☆
25							☆☆☆☆☆

At-A-Glance Records

Run	Date	Distance	Time	Pace	Av. HR	Kcal	Satisfaction
26							☆☆☆☆☆
27							☆☆☆☆☆
28							☆☆☆☆☆
29							☆☆☆☆☆
30							☆☆☆☆☆
31							☆☆☆☆☆
32							☆☆☆☆☆
33							☆☆☆☆☆
34							☆☆☆☆☆
35							☆☆☆☆☆
36							☆☆☆☆☆
37							☆☆☆☆☆
38							☆☆☆☆☆
39							☆☆☆☆☆
40							☆☆☆☆☆
41							☆☆☆☆☆
42							☆☆☆☆☆
43							☆☆☆☆☆
44							☆☆☆☆☆
45							☆☆☆☆☆
46							☆☆☆☆☆
47							☆☆☆☆☆
48							☆☆☆☆☆
49							☆☆☆☆☆
50							☆☆☆☆☆

At-A-Glance Records

Run	Date	Distance	Time	Pace	Av. HR	Kcal	Satisfaction
51							☆☆☆☆☆
52							☆☆☆☆☆
53							☆☆☆☆☆
54							☆☆☆☆☆
55							☆☆☆☆☆
56							☆☆☆☆☆
57							☆☆☆☆☆
58							☆☆☆☆☆
59							☆☆☆☆☆
60							☆☆☆☆☆
61							☆☆☆☆☆
62							☆☆☆☆☆
63							☆☆☆☆☆
64							☆☆☆☆☆
65							☆☆☆☆☆
66							☆☆☆☆☆
67							☆☆☆☆☆
68							☆☆☆☆☆
69							☆☆☆☆☆
70							☆☆☆☆☆
71							☆☆☆☆☆
72							☆☆☆☆☆
73							☆☆☆☆☆
74							☆☆☆☆☆
75							☆☆☆☆☆

At-A-Glance Records

Run	Date	Distance	Time	Pace	Av. HR	Kcal	Satisfaction
76							☆☆☆☆☆
77							☆☆☆☆☆
78							☆☆☆☆☆
79							☆☆☆☆☆
80							☆☆☆☆☆
81							☆☆☆☆☆
82							☆☆☆☆☆
83							☆☆☆☆☆
84							☆☆☆☆☆
85							☆☆☆☆☆
86							☆☆☆☆☆
87							☆☆☆☆☆
88							☆☆☆☆☆
89							☆☆☆☆☆
90							☆☆☆☆☆
91							☆☆☆☆☆
92							☆☆☆☆☆
93							☆☆☆☆☆
94							☆☆☆☆☆
95							☆☆☆☆☆
96							☆☆☆☆☆
97							☆☆☆☆☆
98							☆☆☆☆☆
99							☆☆☆☆☆
100							☆☆☆☆☆

After 100 Runs - Reflections

What would you say were your preferred weather conditions when you ran?

What time of the day best suited your runs?

During the last 100 runs, was there anything that helped improve your times?

Was there anything you found which made your running more difficult?

Apart from your footwear, what item could you NOT be without now?

How did you overcome those 'ugh!' days before setting out for a run?

After 100 Runs - Reflections

Over the last 100 runs, which part of your life has benefited the most?

What do you think could be your 'Achilles Heel'?

And what do you think is now your strongest area?

Are you motivated to enter runs such as 10k's, half-marathons or full marathons in the future. If so, what are your plans and expectations.?

My Main Equipment

	Brand #1	Brand #2	Brand #3
Footwear			
Shorts			
Base-layer			
Long Sleeved Top			
Leg-wear			
Vest/T-shirt			
Gloves			
Socks			
Jackets			
Head-wear			
Underwear			
Sweatbands			
Sports Watch			
Phone Apps			
Water Bottle			
Energy Gel			
Energy Drink			
Running Belt			
Phone/Mp3 Player			
Other Gear			